• MEET •
EDVARD MUNCH

Read With You
Center for Excellence in STEAM Education

Read With You

Published by Read With You Publishing. Printed in the United States of America.

ISBN: 979-8-88618-289-7
First Edition December 2022

What's this? Who am I?
What's your name?
Mine is Edvard Munch.

I'm a famous Norwegian painter.
Have you heard of me?

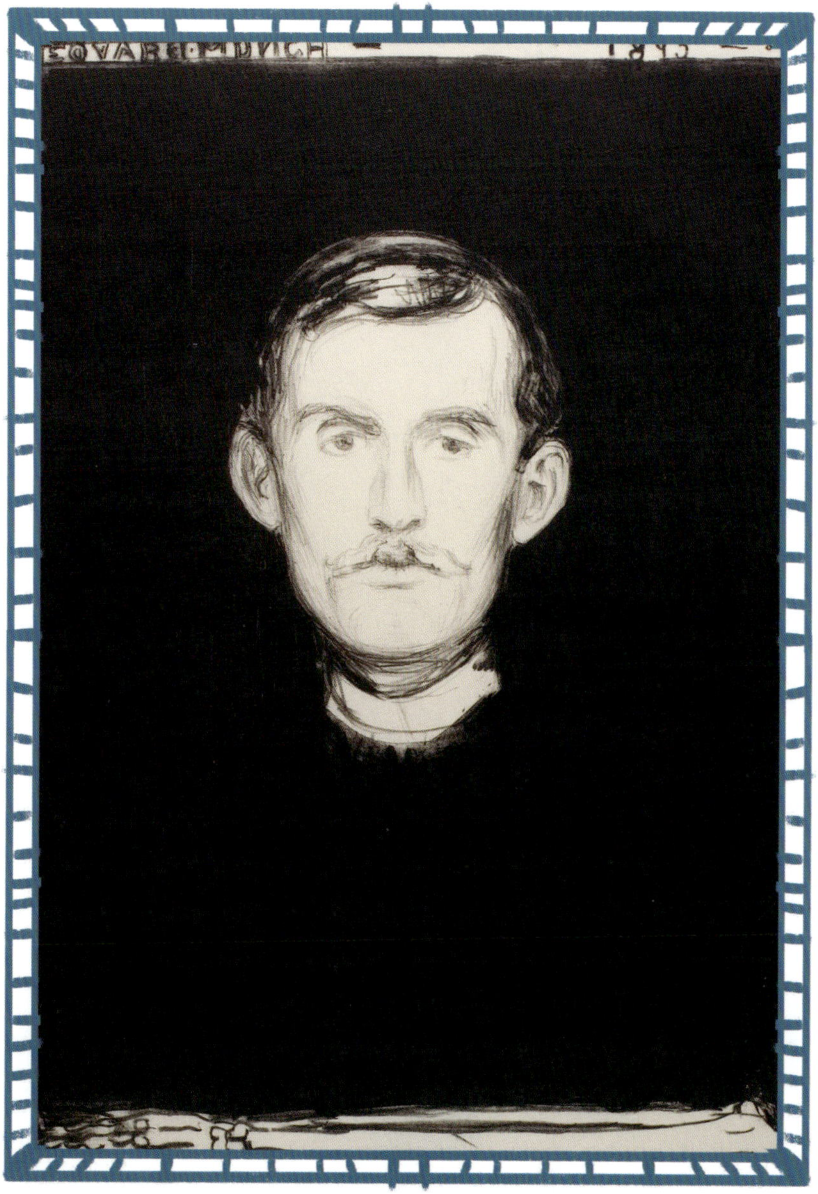

Self Portrait, 1895

My life was difficult, but luckily I had wonderful teachers! Who has taught you the most?

One of my teachers was Hans Jaeger. He taught me to paint how I feel. How do you think I felt when I drew this?

Two Human Beings. The Lonely Ones, 1894

There is a word for the art style where you paint your emotions, or what you feel. It's called *Expressionism*.

Expressionists show emotion through pictures. Maybe if I am sad, I paint a blue picture. If I am happy, I paint a yellow picture.

The Girls on the Bridge, 1918

We can also paint a picture with no color at all! What could be near this floor?

What might the man by the window be thinking about?

Moonlight. Night in Saint Cloud, 1895

I like to make paintings that don't look realistic. What colors and lines can you find here?

My mother and sister passed away when I was little, and my father was very strict. So, I liked to live in my imagination where life was happier.

Young Woman on the Beach, 1896

Another painter who paints creatively is my friend and teacher Vincent van Gogh. This swirled line is similar to his brushstrokes!

What emotion does this painting make you feel? Check the title to see if you felt what I was feeling when I painted this!

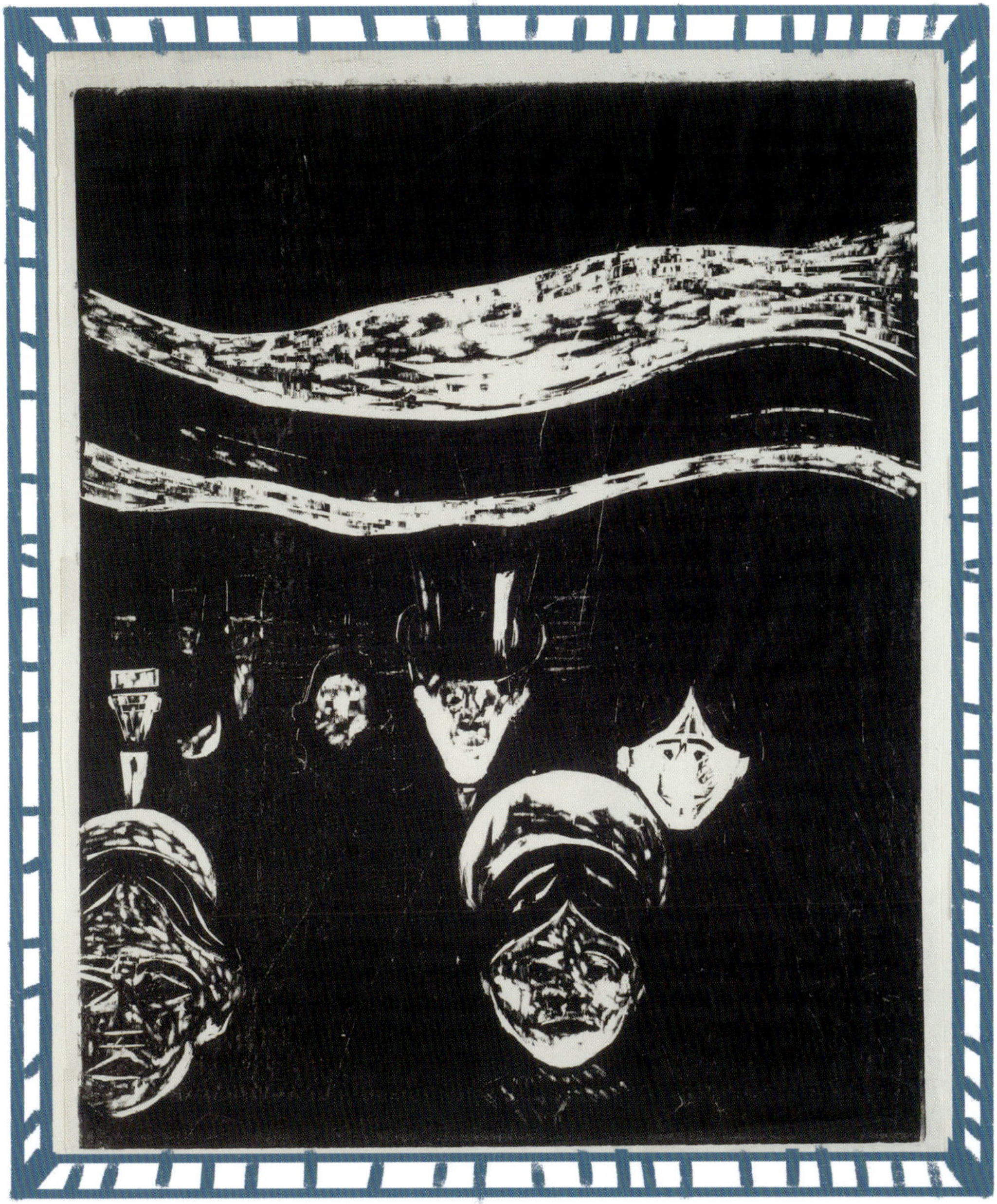

Anxiety, 1896

This is the background of my most famous Expressionist painting. I came up with the idea when I was walking as the sun set one evening.

I thought I heard the scream of nature all around me, so I painted a scream to match my feelings!

The Scream, 1895

Sometimes, it's easier to express yourself with paint than with words. Try using colors to explain what's inside you!

Self-Portrait in Moonlight, 1904–1906

Find Examples

This painting is *Melancholy III*, 1902.

Study the picture. What do you think melancholy means?

What colors did Munch choose to show the man's feelings?

Do you think the man in the painting is Edvard Munch or someone else?

If this painting were called Joy, how would it look different?

Connect

This painting is *Girl by the Window*, 1893.

Have you ever been so sick that you couldn't go outside to play?

Munch was often sick as a child. Why might he have painted so many pictures of people standing by windows?

What could you add to this picture to change its feeling?

How would Munch's paintings look differently if he lived today?

Craft

Option 1

1. Close your eyes and think of how you are feeling. What colors and objects show that feeling?

2. Grab a pencil and draw your feelings!

Option 2

1. Hold the page with *The Scream* up to a window and trace the person onto the bottom of a blank sheet of paper.

2. Think of something scary. It could be dinosaurs, big robots, broccoli, or anything else!

3. Draw that scary thing behind the person.

4. Now you have your own version of the portrait! Show it to your friends and ask them what scary thing they might add.

Explore fun facts about interesting painters by visiting
https://www.readwithyou.com/pages/meet-the-artist-activities